Published by Cypress Hills Press
Brooklyn, New York

Book design: Richard Tackett
http://www.richtackett.com

2

HOW GREEN WAS MY VALLEY ON FILM & TV

BY
SCOTT PALMER

INTRODUCTION

This is a reference book about the film and television adaptations of *How Green Was My Valley*. The book includes the 1941 film and two B.B.C. television adaptations, in 1960 and 1975-6. It includes complete cast listings, numerous photographs, directorial credits, and a story synopsis for each presentation.

How Green Was My Valley was first a 1941 American motion picture directed by John Ford. It was based on the best-selling novel of the same name by Richard Llewellyn.

The film, set in the late Victorian era, depicts a small Welsh coal mining village and specifically the Morgan family, with its father, mother, six sons and one daughter. The story is told as seen through the eyes of the youngest son, Huw Morgan.

The film starred Walter Pidgeon, Maureen O'Hara, Donald Crisp, Roddy McDowall, Anna Lee and Barry Fitzgerald, and won five Academy Awards, including Best Film, Best Director (John Ford) and Best Supporting Actor (Donald Crisp).

How Green Was My Valley was next made as a television series for B.B.C. One, running eight episodes between January 1, 1960, and February 19th. It was faithful to the original novel.

Finally, in 1975, a six part B.B.C. TV serial began showing on December 29, 1975, and culminated on February 2, 1976. Set in South Wales during the reign of Queen Victoria, the story of the Morgans, a mining family, is told.

The story centers around Huw, the youngest boy, whose academic ability enables him to consider a future away from the mines in which his father and five brothers toil. Huw has a life-changing experience after his father is trapped in a mine cave-in.

The series starred Sir Stanley Baker (who unfortunately died in 1976) and Sean Phillips, both of whom won critical acclaim for their roles as the heads of the Morgan family. The series was co-produced by 20th Century Fox, who owned the rights to the novel; Fox had also produced the original motion picture.

TABLE OF CONTENTS:

1941: How Green Was My Valley (Film)

1960: How Green Was My Valley 8 Part Series

1975-76 How Green Was My Valley 6 Part Series

HOW GREEN WAS MY VALLEY (1941)

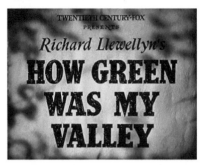

DIRECTED BY JOHN FORD
PRODUCED BY DARRYL F. ZANUCK
WRITTEN BY PHILIP DUNNE
ORIGINAL NOVEL BY RICHARD LLEWELLYN

CAST

Walter Pidgeon................Mr. Gruffyd
Maureen O'Hara.................Angharad
Roddy McDowall..........Huw Morgan
Donald Crisp............Gwilym Morgan
Sara Allgood...................Beth Morgan
Anna Lee................................Bronwyn
John Loder......................Ianto Morgan
Barry Fitzgerald.....................Cyfartha
Patric Knowles................Ivor Morgan
Rhys Williams....................Dai Bando
Morton Lowry.....................Mr. Jonas
Arthur Shields.......................Mr. Parry
Frederic Worlock............Dr. Richards
Richard Fraser...............Davy Morgan
Evan S. Evans......Gwilym Morgan Jr.
James Monks...............Owen Morgan
Ethel Griffies................Mrs. Nicholas
Lionel Pape.........................Mr. Evans

Walter Pidgeon   Maureen O'Hara

Roddy McDowall   Donald Crisp

Sara Allgood   Anna Lee

Marten Lamont...............Ieston Evans
Clifford Severn..........Mervyn Phillips
Eve March...................Meillyn Lewis
Ann Todd.............................Ceinwen
Herbert Evans........................Postman
Mary Field.................................Eve
Jack Pennick......Mine Superintendent
Mary Gordon...........................Gossip
Tiny Jones.........................Mrs. Tossel
Louis Jean Heydt.......................Miner
Mae Marsh.....................Miner's Wife
Irving Pichel...Older Huw Morgan(voice)
Harry McKim, Lydia McKim, Peggy
McKim.................................Children
Victor Adamson, C.E. Anderson,
George Atkinson, Ted Billings, Nora
Bush, Ruth Clifford, Jane Crowley,
Jack Curtis, Michael Jeffers, Jack
Kenny, Al Kunde, Merrill McCor-
mick, Leslie Sketchley, Harry Ten-
brook, Dorothy Vernon, Eleanore Vo-
gel......................................Villagers

AND: Gertrude Astor, Stewart Bair,
Frank Baker, Robert Bradford, Cyril
Clare, Leonard Clare, Philip Dare,
Edward Davies, Helen Davies, Minta
Durfee, Pauline Garon, Gibson Gow-
land, Jack Griffiths, Ben Hall, Gwi-
lym Isaac, Ellis James, Alice Jones,
Arvonia Jones, David Jones, Emlyn
Jones, Howell Jones, Joseph Jones,
Will Lewis, Ann McCullough, Gomer

John Loder   Barry Fitzgerald

Patric Knowles   Rhys Williams

Morton Lowry   Arthur Shields

Frederic Worlock   Richard Fraser

Evan S. Evans   James Monks

Ethel Griffies   Lionel Pape

Morgan, Jack Owen, Arthur Pritchard, David J. Reed, Caradac Rees, Lewis Rees, Hugh Thomas, John C. Thomas, Owen Thomas, Allan Watson, Jan Williams, Reese Williams, Robert B. Williams, Tudor Williams

Marten Lamont

Clifford Severn

Eve March

Ann Todd

Herbert Evans

Mary Field

Jack Pennick

Mary Gordon

Tiny Jones

Louis Jean Heydt

Mae Marsh

Harry Tenbrook

Gertrude Astor

Minta Durfee

Gibson Gowland

The film begins with a monologue by an older Huw Morgan: "I am packing my belongings in the shawl my mother used to wear when she went to the market, and I'm going from my valley. And this time, I shall never return."

We then flash back to a time when Huw was about 12 years old; the youngest child of Gwilym Morgan, Huw walks home with his father to meet his mother, Beth Morgan.

Anna Lee, Sara Allgood, Maureen O'Hara

Richard Fraser, Donald Crisp. Maureen O'Hara, James Monks, Evan S. Evans, John Loder

Barry Fitzgerald, Rhys Williams

Roddy McDowall as Huw Morgan

His older brothers, Ianto, Ivor, Davy, Gwilym Jr., and Owen all work in the local coal mines with their father, while sister Angharad keeps house with their mother.

Huw had a happy childhood for the most part, the valley lovely and green, and not yet spoiled from soot from the mines; the Morgan home is warm and friendly.

The men, almost all miners, are content in their work, bursting into song on the way home. After washing off the coal dust, the family eats together, with father Gwilym Morgan at the head of the table.

Huw mentions that while his father may be the head of the family, his mother was it's heart. The wages are collected, the men wash then eat together. Afterwards the spending money is given out.

Barry Fitzgerald & Rhys Williams

Morton Lowry, Rhys Williams

Maureen O'Hara, Roddy McDowall

Donald Crisp, Roddy McDowall, Sara Allgood

13

Clifford Severn, Roddy McDowall

Walter Pidgeon, James Monks, John Loder

Donald Crisp, James Monks, Richard Fraser, Evan S. Evans,
John Loder

Maureen O'Hara, Sara Allgood

A marriage is arranged between Ivor Morgan, Huw's eldest
brother, and a girl from a neighbouring valley named Bronwyn. When she arrives in the town, Huw immediately falls
in love with the beautiful young woman.

At the marriage party, the new minister, Mr. Gruffyd, pre-
sides; he and Angharad, Huw's sister, are immediately attracted to one another. Mr. Parry, a deacon of the church,
accuses Gruffyd of practicing Socialism when the preacher
sides with Morgan's sons regarding forming a union.

15

Rhys Williams, Barry Fitzgerald, Donald Crisp, Roddy McDowall,
James Monks, John Loder

Donald Crisp, Sara Allgood

Mr. Jonas knocked unconscious

Arthur Shields as Mr. Parry

Soon afterwards, the mine owners decrease the worker's wages, forcing more men from other valleys to look for work. Now with so many men willing to work for less money, trouble is on the horizon.

The Morgan brothers become disgruntled too; a heated discussion arises at the dinner table. Gwilym says that the table is a place for eating and not talking about these problems.

But one of his sons says that if they can treat Gwilym Morgan, a mining foreman with seniority in such a cavalier fashion, what will happen to the other men? Gwilym again asks them not to speak.

Young Davy says he will speak about injustice anywhere he sees fit. His father says he should have better manners. Ianto replies "We are not questioning your authority sir, but if manners prevent us from speaking the truth, we shall be without manners."

Maureen O'Hara & Walter Pidgeon

Roddy McDowall, Walter Pidgeon

John Loder, Richard Fraser, Roddy McDowall

Walter Pidgeon as Mr. Gruffydd

Coal miners walking home

Notice posted at the colliery

Donald Crisp, Sara Allgood

Sara Allgood, Maureen O'Hara, Donald Crisp

The four brothers leave not only the table, but the house as well, taking up lodgings in the village. Huw is left alone with his father, who is obviously distressed. When Huw makes a noise, Gwilym responds "Yes my son, I know you are there."

The men go on strike. The town is full out unemployed men, who are in an ugly mood. Because Gwilym Morgan opposed the strike, he is seen as a traitor by some. It's not long before a rock is thrown through the Morgan's front window.

Late that snowy night, Beth Morgan, accompanied by Huw, attends a meeting of the strikers, defending her husband's thinking and saying that if any harm comes to Gwilym, she will find who is responsible and kill them with her bare hands.

She grabs Huw and they head for home; unfortunately they fall into an icy bog. They are pulled out by some of the men, but both of them have lost the use of their legs due to frostbite. Dr. Richards says that Huw may never walk again. But Mr. Gruffyd works with Huw, both mentally and physically, and eventually he (as well as Mrs. Morgan) are able to walk normally again. Gruffyd's hard work and care endear him to the Morgan family-especially Angharad.

Walter Pidgeon, Roddy McDowall

John Loder, Roddy McDowall, Evan S. Evans, James Monks, Richard Fraser, Patric Knowles, Donald Crisp

Anna Lee with baby

Gwilym Morgan at the dinner table

Sara Allgood, Anna Lee

Huw sits alone at the table

Evan S. Evans, Donald Crisp

The strike is eventually settled, and Gwilym and his sons reconcile, yet many miners have lost their jobs. Angharad is courted by the mine owner's son, Iestyn Evans, though she loves Mr. Gruffydd.

Mr. Gruffydd loves her too, to the malicious delight of the gossipy townswomen, but cannot bear to subject her to an impoverished churchman's life. Angharad submits to a love-less marriage to Evans, and they move out of the country.

Next, Huw is accepted into a school in a valley a few miles away. He gets off to a bad start by arriving late with muddy boots. Mr. Jonas, the teacher, is a sadist who delights in humiliating Huw.

The other boys treat him roughly, especially Mervyn Phillips, who breaks Huw's pencil box, then beats the hell out of him. When a bloodied Huw returns home, his father actually encourages him to fight, going so far as to get the help of former boxer Dai Bando and his friend Cyfartha to teach Huw how to fight properly.

Evan S. Evans, Richard Fraser, Maureen O'Hara, James Monks, John Loder

Anna Lee, Patric Knowles

26

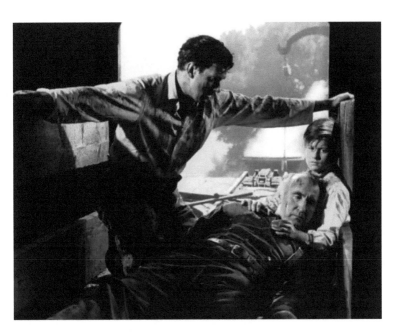

Walter Pidgeon, Donald Crisp, Roddy McDowall

Maureen O'Hara, Walter Pidgeon

Maureen O'Hara, Donald Crisp, Anna Lee

Barry Fitzgerald, right, as Cyfartha

The Morgan brothers leave home

Lobby Card

Sara Allgood, Roddy McDowall, Donald Crisp

James Monks as Owen Morgan

Patric Knowles & Anna Lee

When he becomes proficient, Huw challenges Mervyn-and beats him. Unfortunately Mr. Jonas sees this, and canes Huw so savagely that the flesh is ripped from his back.

Returning home, an injured Huw is greeted by his brother, along with Cyfartha and Dai Bando. The men are horrified by Huw's condition, but Huw says he broke the rules by fighting. He tells them to leave Jonas alone. But Dai Bando and Cyfartha have other ideas.

The two men appear at the school the next day; Jonas asks what they want and Dai Bando replies "Knowledge." He asks Jonas how to measure a stick, to which the teacher replies "By its length, of course."

"And how would you measure a man who would use a stick on a boy one-third his size?" asks the boxer-who then goes on to backhand Jonas across the face, sending him to the floor.

Donald Crisp, Roddy McDowall, Walter Pidgeon

Donald Crisp, Roddy McDowall

Patric Knowles & Donald Crisp

Lobby Card

33

Donald Crisp as Gwilym Morgan

Explosion in the mine

Anna Lee as Bronwen

Lobby Card

35

Film Poster

Film Poster

While Cyfartha picks Jonas up, Dai Bando addresses the children: "Could I have your attention, boys and girls? I am not accustomed to speaking in public." "Only public houses," says Cyfartha.

"But this," says Dai Bando, smashing Jonas in the nose "never use. It's against the rules-break a man's nose. Now then..." Jonas is now sitting against the wall, unconscious. "I'm afraid he will never make a boxer," Dai Bando says. "No aptitude for knowledge," replies Cyfartha.

On the day that Bronwyn gives birth to their child, Ivor is killed in a mine accident. Later, two of Morgan's sons are dismissed in favor of less experienced, cheaper laborers.

With no job, they leave to seek their fortunes in America. Huw is awarded a scholarship to university, but to his father's dismay he refuses it to work in the mines. He relocates with Bronwyn, to help provide for her and her child.

Patric Knowles leads the choir

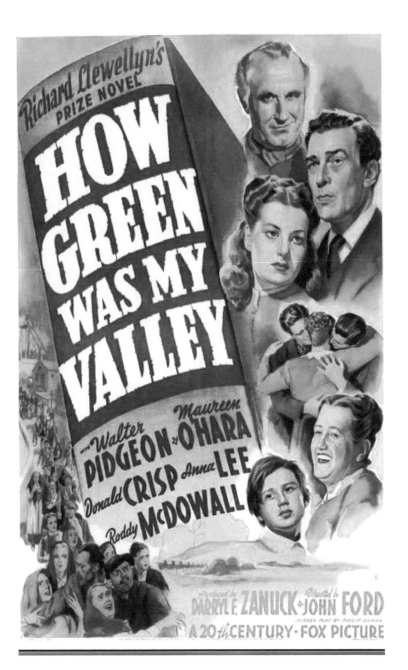

Film Poster

Lobby Card

Donald Crisp studying a problem

Foreign Film Poster

When Angharad returns without her husband, vicious gossip of an impending divorce spreads through the town. Mr. Gruffydd is denounced by the church deacons, and after condemning the town's narrow-mindedness, he decides to leave. When Huw tells his mother Angharad has done nothing wrong, Beth replies "Nothing is enough for people who have minds like cesspools." Just then, the alarm whistle sounds, signalling another mine disaster. Several men are injured, and Gwilym and others are trapped in a cave-in far underground-where it is beginning to flood.

Huw, Mr. Gruffydd, and Dai Bando descend with others for a rescue attempt. Huw finds his father, trapped under a large boulder. He puts his arms around Huw, then dies. Huw rides the lift to the surface cradling his father's body.

Foreign Film Poster

Foreign Film Poster

Back in the present, the older Huw recalls, "Men like my father cannot die. They are with me still, real in memory as they were in flesh, loving and beloved forever. How green was my valley then." Huw then thinks of his time when he was a boy once more.

How Green Was My Valley was based on the best-selling 1939 novel by Richard Llewellyn. The fictional village in the film is based on Gilfach Goch, where Llewellyn spent many summers visiting his grandfather, and it served as the inspiration for the novel.

It was nominated for ten Oscars, winning for Best Picture, Best Director (John Ford), Best Supporting Actor (Donald Crisp), Best Cinematography, and Best Art Direction.

Roddy McDowall with a slice of bread

HOW GREEN WAS MY VALLEY (1960)

EPISODE 1: THE FIRST RIFT

DIRECTED BY Dafydd Gruffyd   ORIGINAL AIR DATE: January 1, 1960

CAST

Eynon Evans............Gwilym Morgan
Rachel Thomas..............Beth Morgan
Glyn Houston................Davy Morgan
David Lyn.......................Ivor Morgan
Hugh David.................Owen Morgan
Emrys James........Gwilym Morgan Jr.
Sulwen Morgan.....Angharad Morgan
Islwyn Maelor Evans.....Huw Morgan
Margaret John.......................Bronwen
T.H. Evans......................Dr. Richards
Emrys Cleaver.......................Minister
Howell Evans, Brinley Jenkins..Miner

Eynon Evans   Rachel Thomas

Glyn Houston   David Lyn

Hugh David   Emrys James

Margaret John   Emrys Cleaver   Howell Evans   Brinley Jenkins

45

In this episode, Davy Morgan attends a meeting on the mountain with fateful results for the Morgan family.

Margaret John, David Lyn

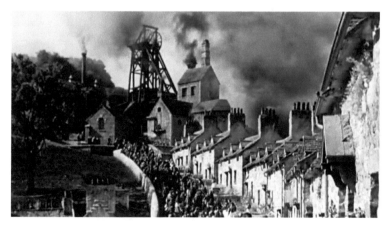

View of the village

EPISODE 2: THE NEW MINISTER

DIRECTED BY Dafydd Gruffyd   ORIGINAL AIR DATE: January 8, 1960

CAST

William Squire........Merddyn Gruffyd
Eynon Evans............Gwilym Morgan
Rachel Thomas..............Beth Morgan
Islwyn Maelor Evans.....Huw Morgan
Glyn Houston................Davy Morgan
Emrys James........Gwilym Morgan Jr.
Hugh David..................Owen Morgan
June Lewis...................Marged Evans
Glanffrwd James...............John Evans
Peter Lawrence.........Idris the Barman

William Squire

Eynon Evans

Rachel Thomas

Glyn Houston

Emrys James

Hugh David

Peter Lawrence

The Reverend Merddyn Gruffyd comes to the valley, and Huw's life takes a new turn.

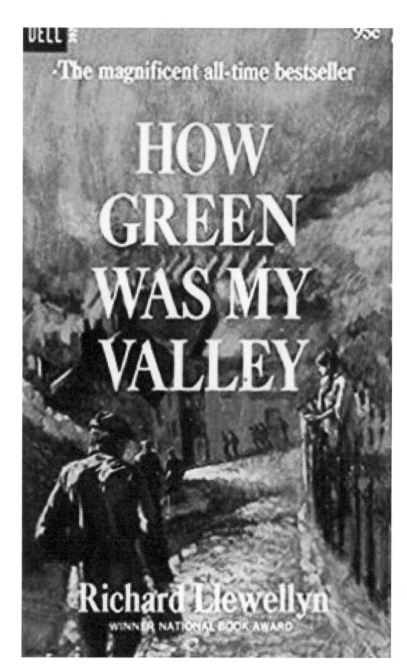

Book Cover

EPISODE 3: THE NATIONAL SCHOOL

The National School

DIRECTED BY Dafydd Gruffyd   ORIGINAL AIR DATE: January 15, 1960

CAST

Islwyn Maelor Evans.....Huw Morgan
William Squire.................Mr. Gruffyd
Sulwen Morgan...................Angharad
Eynon Evans............Gwilym Morgan
Rachel Thomas..............Beth Morgan
Dillwyn Owen.....................Mr. Jonas
Dudley Owen............Mervyn Phillips
Anita Morgan..........Cienwen Phillips
Emrys James........Gwilym Morgan Jr.
Glyn Houston................Davy Morgan
Hugh David..................Owen Morgan
Edward Rees...................Mr. Motshill
Michael Forrest..................Dai Bando
W.H. Williams............Cyfartha Lewis
June Lewis..............................Marged

AND: Jean Brown, Marion Davies, Paul Hardy, Lesley Hughes, Myfanwy Jones, Geoffrey Lacy, Timothy Williams

William Squire

Eynon Evans

Rachel Thomas

Dillwyn Owen

Emrys James

Glyn Houston

Hugh David

Michael Forrest

49

Huw goes to school for the first time, and makes new friends as well as new enemies.

Huw with Mr. Gruffydd

EPISODE 4: FURTHER EDUCATION

Further
Education

DIRECTED BY Dafydd Gruffyd   ORIGINAL AIR DATE: January 22, 1960

CAST

William Squire.................Mr. Gruffyd
Rachel Thomas..............Beth Morgan
Islwyn Maelor Evans.....Huw Morgan
Sulwen Morgan...................Angharad
Eynon Evans............Gwilym Morgan
Glyn Houston................Davy Morgan
Conrad Evans.......................Mr. Parry
Anita Morgan..........Ceinwen Phillips
Dudley Owen............Mervyn Phillips
Dillwyn Owen......................Mr. Jonas
Michael Forrest.................Dai Bando
W.H. Williams............Cyfartha Lewis
Edward Rees...................Mr. Motshill

AND: Jean Brown, Marion Davies, Paul Hardy, Lesley Hughes, Myfanwy Jones, Geoffrey Lacy, Timothy Williams

William Squire

Rachel Thomas

Eynon Evans

Glyn Houston

Dillwyn Owen   Michael Forrest

Mr. Gruffyd falls foul of the deacons, Huw listens to nightingales, and Dai Bando gives his views on education.

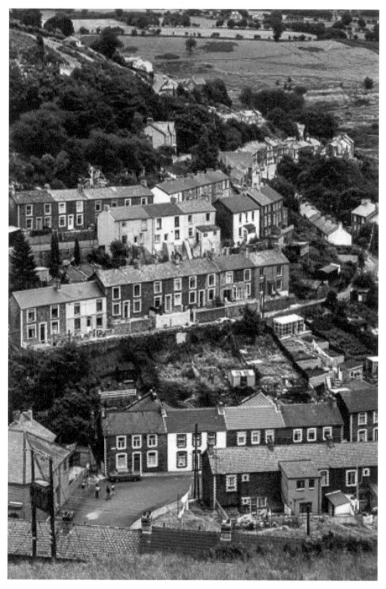

Overhead view of the town

EPISODE 5: PROPOSAL AND DISPOSAL

Proposal and Disposal

DIRECTED BY Dafydd Gruffyd   ORIGINAL AIR DATE: January 29 1960

CAST

Glyn Houston................Davy Morgan
Henley Thomas..............Huw Morgan
William Squire................Mr. Gruffyd
Sulwen Morgan...................Angharad
Rachel Thomas..............Beth Morgan
Eynon Evans............Gwilym Morgan
Desmond Llewelyn.............Mr. Evans
Ray Smith.......................Iestyn Evans
Anita Morgan..........Cienwen Phillips
Margaret John.......................Bronwen
David Lyn.......................Ivor Morgan

Glyn Houston   Henley Thomas

William Squire   Rachel Thomas

Eynon Evans   Desmond Llewelyn

Ray Smith   Margaret John   David Lyn

53

In this episode, Huw grows up, Angharad receives a proposal, and Mr. Gruffyd makes his position clear.

Miners are out of work

EPISODE 6: NEW LIVES FOR OLD

New Lives for Old

DIRECTED BY Dafydd Gruffyd   ORIGINAL AIR DATE: February 5, 1960

CAST

Henley Thomas..............Huw Morgan
Margaret John......................Bronwen
Eynon Evans............Gwilym Morgan
Glyn Houston................Davy Morgan
William Squire.................Mr. Gruffyd
Sulwen Morgan...................Angharad
Rachel Thomas..............Beth Morgan
David Lyn.......................Ivor Morgan
Michael Forrest..................Dai Bando
Anita Morgan..........Cienwen Phillips
Madoline Thomas........Mrs. Nicholas
Ray Smith.......................Iestyn Evans
Christine Pollon.........Blodwen Evans

Henley Thomas   Margaret John

Eynon Evans   Glyn Houston

William Squire   Rachel Thomas

David Lyn   Michael Forrest   Madoline Thomas   Ray Smith   Christine Pollon

Angharad makes her choice, and Davy finds something more interesting than unions.

Angharad on the hillside

EPISODE 7: NEW WAYS OF LIVING

DIRECTED BY Dafydd Gruffyd   ORIGINAL AIR DATE: February 12, 1960

CAST

Eynon Evans............Gwilym Morgan
Rachel Thomas..............Beth Morgan
Margaret John.......................Bronwen
Henley Thomas..............Huw Morgan
Glyn Houston.................Davy Morgan
Madoline Thomas.........Mrs. Nicholas
Christine Pollon.........Blodwen Evans
Sulwen Morgan...................Angharad
William Squire................Mr. Gruffyd
Madge Jones....................Mrs. Davies

AND: Sally Havard, Kate Jones, Evan
Morgan, Jack Walters

Eynon Evans

Rachel Thomas

Margaret John

Henley Thomas

Glyn Houston

Madoline Thomas

Christine Pollon

William Squire

In this episode, Angharad returns to the valley, and both Huw and Mr. Gruffyd defy convention.

Men coming home from work

EPISODE 8: THE LAST RIFT

DIRECTED BY Dafydd Gruffyd ORIGINAL AIR DATE: February 19, 1960

CAST

Henley Thomas..............Huw Morgan
Margaret John.....................Bronwen
Eynon Evans............Gwilym Morgan
William Squire................Mr. Gruffyd
Brinley Jenkins...............Matt Herries
Michael Forrest..................Dai Bando
W.H. Williams............Cyfartha Lewis
Rachel Thomas..............Beth Morgan
Clyde Pollitt...........................Agitator

Henley Thomas

Margaret John

Eynon Evans

William Squire

Brinley Jenkins

Michael Forrest

Rachel Thomas

Clyde Pollitt

An explosion at the mine

HOW GREEN WAS MY VALLEY (1975)
EPISODE 1: HILLTOP WALK

DIRECTED BY Ronald Wilson ORIGINAL AIR DATE: December 29, 1975

CAST

Stanley Baker...........Gwilym Morgan
Sian Phillips...................Beth Morgan
Nerys Hughes.........Bronwen Morgan
Norman Comer................Ifor Morgan
Keith Drinkel................Ianto Morgan
Mike Gwilym..............Owen Morgan
Sue Jones-Davies...Angharad Morgan
Huw Justin.....................Huw Morgan
Rhys Powys...................Huw Morgan
Gareth Thomas....Reverend Gruffydd
Victoria Plucknett........Marged Evans
Ray Smith..........................Dai Bando
John Clive.............................Cyfartha
Aubrey Richards.........................Elias
Eric Francis..........................Mr. Price
Clive Roberts.............................Miner
Dudley Jones......................Mr. Evans
Elizabeth Stewart..............Mrs. Evans
Maureen Williams.......Miellyn Lewis

Stanley Baker

Sian Phillips

Nerys Hughes

Norman Comer

Keith Drinkel

Mike Gwilym

Sue Jones-Davies   Huw Justin

Rhys Powys   Gareth Thomas   Victoria Plucknett   Ray Smith   John Clive   Aubrey Richards

Eric Francis   Clive Roberts   Dudley Jones   Elizabeth Stewart   Maureen Williams   Villager

Young Huw Morgan and his mother are walking along in the country when Mrs. Morgan stumbles and falls to the edge of the precipice. She holds on near the top.

When Huw tries to rescue his mother, he falls too, tumbling all the way down to the bottom, landing in some water. Luckily his father Gwilym is nearby and goes to get the boy, carrying him home.

Keith Drinkel & Mike Gwilym

Norman Comer, Keith Drinkel, Mike Gwilym

Mike Gwilym, Stanley Baker

Norman Comer, Nerys Hughes, Eric Francis

Sian Phillips, Stanley Baker, Eric Francis

Dudley Jones, Victoria Plucknett

Keith Drinkel, Victoria Plucknett, Dudley Jones, Mike Gwilym

Huw is injured, and confined to bed. The following Sunday, the Morgan family, sans Huw, attends chapel which is presided over by the new minister, Mr. Gruffydd.

The Morgan family consists of Mr. and Mrs. Morgan, the aforementioned Huw, and three grown boys, Ivor, Ianto, and Owen, as well as daughter Angharad.

Ivor brings a young woman named Bronwen Price home to meet his family, along with her father. Bronwen and Ivor become engaged and soon are married. Everyone is happy about that.

Rhys Powys, Sian Phillips

Keith Drinkel, Ray Smith, John Clive, Eric Francis

Huw Justin, Sian Phillips

Ray Smith & Keith Drinkel

Aubrey Richards, Gareth Thomas

Aubrey Richards points his finger

Gruffydd begins visiting Huw, and when he asks when Huw will be able to walk again, Mrs. Morgan says that the doctor stated that nature will have to take its course. Gruffydd says that nature is the handmaiden of the Lord.

Stanley Baker, Sian Phillips

Keith Drinkel, Sue Jones-Davies, Mike Gwilym, Rhys Powys

A joyous Mr. Morgan comes home with the newspaper to announce that Huw has been awarded first prize in a writing competition. Brother Ianto then gives Huw a job writing letters on behalf of the union.

Aubrey Richards, Rhys Powys

Victoria Plucknett, Keith Drinkel

Brother Owen begins mouthing off at the supper table about the problems at the colliery, where they all work. This upsets his father. The dinner table is no place for rudeness.

With the support of Ivor and Ianto, Owen leaves the table, and the three of them decide to leave the house. Angharad says she will go too, to look after them. Mrs. Morgan says no, but Angharad goes anyway.

The boys find lodgings at a squalid boarding house. But after a short time there, they decide to come home. Mr. Morgan tells them everyone-including him-will now be considered lodgers, as he feels he gets no respect from his sons.

Sian Phillips, Stanley Baker

Norman Comer, Eric Francis

With the help of Mr. Gruffydd, Huw is able to start walking, and goes up a nearby hill to pick some daffodils for his
mother. His overcoming his leg problems gives the entire
family reason to rejoice.

A local girl, Marged Evans, has been living at the Morgan
home since the boys went away. Owen is attracted to her.
He says he loves her face, her voice, and everything about
her. He proposes and she accepts.

Next, Ivor and Bronwen are married by Mr. Gruffydd. Mrs.
Morgan says she will miss her son, even though the couple
will only be living six houses away.

At the reception at the Morgan home, Mr. Evans and Owen
indulge in a screaming match and nearly come to blows
when he sees Owen kissing Marged. When she tells him
they are to marry, Evans calms down.

73

Later, the self-righteous Mr. Elias says that the Morgans and their guests are blasphemers, singing and drinking at such a late hour on the Sabbath Day. Gruffydd tells Elias he is a sanctimonious prig, and throws him out.

Owen seems to be having second thoughts about Marged-she is too open and friendly-not like the girl who married dear old dad. Marged confides in Ianto, who says that Owen is a bloody fool.

After the next chapel meeting, Elias castigates Meillyn Lewis, who has given birth to an illegitimate baby. Huw is nearby, and when he hears, tears a strip off Elias for being cruel to the girl.

Now Huw is in trouble-but not with his mother. Beth Morgan is proud of her son for standing up for what he thinks is right and telling off a bunch of old hypocrites.

Mr. Morgan says that Huw should not have interfered, as well as telling his wife "Now I know why I am living in a nest of scorpions-it's you!" Gwilym and Beth smile at each other.

Stanley Baker, Gareth Thomas

EPISODE 2: NEW ARRIVALS

DIRECTED BY Ronald Wilson   ORIGINAL AIR DATE: January 5, 1976

CAST

Stanley Baker...........Gwilym Morgan
Sian Phillips...................Beth Morgan
Nerys Hughes.........Bronwen Morgan
Norman Comer...............Ifor Morgan
Keith Drinkel................Ianto Morgan
Mike Gwilym...............Owen Morgan
Sue Jones-Davies...Angharad Morgan
Rhys Powys...................Huw Morgan
Gareth Thomas.....Reverend Gruffydd
Jeremy Clyde...................Iestin Evans
Ray Smith.........................Dai Bando
John Clive...........................Cyfartha
Victoria Plucknett...................Marged
Aubrey Richards.........................Elias
Patricia Mort..................Mrs. Beynon
Clifford Rose.......................Mr. Jonas
Ivor Roberts....................Mr. Motshill
Michael Griffiths.......Mervyn Phillips

Stanley Baker

Sian Phillips

Nerys Hughes

Norman Comer

Keith Drinkel

Mike Gwilym

Sue Jones-Davies   Rhys Powys

Gareth Thomas   Jeremy Clyde   Ray Smith   John Clive   Victoria Plucknett   Aubrey Richards

Patricia Mort   Clifford Rose   Ivor Roberts   Michael Griffiths

While Angharad and her mother help a widowed neighbour lady who is having a baby, Owen and Ianto have harsh words about Marged. Ianto doesn't want to see Marged "mucked about."

Beth and Angharad have collected clothes and food for Mrs. Beynon, and Mr. Gruffydd has even found her a new place to live. Meanwile, Bronwen tells the Morgans she is expecting a baby; Ivor is so happy he is like "a dog with two tails."

John Clive, Ray Smith

Sian Phillips, Stanley Baker

Norman Comer, Nerys Hughes, Sue Jones-Davies

Keith Drinkel, Stanley Baker, Sian Phillips, Norman Comer,
Rhys Powys

Rhys Powys, Stanley Baker, Keith Drinkel

Stanley Baker, Rhys Powys

Marged tells Ianto that she is feeling increasingly uncomfortable living with the Morgans-especially Owen. Ianto says he will marry her, and they can live in the next valley. Marged will think it over, she says.

Mr. Morgan asks Gruffydd if he thinks Huw is ready to return to school. This enrages Ianto; he shouts that the family cannot make any decision with out consulting Gruffydd. Even Angharad thinks the sun shines out of Gruffydd's backside!

Marged and Owen get into a screaming match when she tells him that if he no longer wants her, Ianto does. This makes Owen angry not only at her, but also at his brother Ianto.

Back at Gruffydd's lodgings, Elias appears and tells Gruffydd that he is upset that Angharad Morgan has been chosen to teach Sunday School instead of his sister-in-law.

Gruffydd then tells Elias the reason was that the sister-in-law does not like children, and the children don't like her. Angharad seems to get along with everyone.

After Elias leaves, Ianto shows up and has a heart to heart talk with Gruffydd. The two men put their differences aside and seem to come to a meeting of the minds.

Sue Jones-Davies, Rhys Powys

Keith Drinkel, Stanley Baker

Sue Jones-Davies, Sian Phillips

Stanley Baker, Gareth Thomas

Nerys Hughes, Rhys Powys

Patricia Mort, Sue Jones-Davies

Jeremy Clyde, Sue Jones-Davies

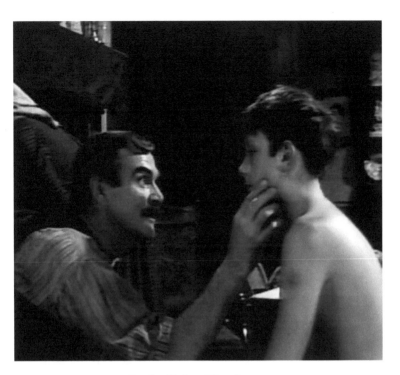

Stanley Baker, Rhys Powys

Marget leaves the Morgan home. She can no longer take the uncomfortable situation. At the mine, Ianto speaks to miner and professional boxer Dai Bando and his friend Cyfartha about mine and union business.

Angharad gets her head stuck in some bars; Mr. Gruffydd comes along and gets her out, cutting his hand. When Angharad applies a bandage, the two realize they have developed feelings for each other.

Mr. and Mrs. Morgan are pleased at their new grandson. After Ianto and Marged are married, Owen tells her that he made a big mistake. He tries to get her to run off with him, but she refuses.

At this time, someone has stolen a number of the Morgan's turkeys. Huw traces a feather to the shop of Mr. Elias-who throws Huw out when he tries to buy some licorice.

Returning home, Huw tells his father, who goes to the shop and confronts Elias. The other three Morgan sons find the turkeys in the rear yard, and recover them. Ianto punches Elias in the mouth.

Huw and Angharad are out walking when they meet Iestyn Evans, son of the mine owner. He is on horseback, and allows Huw to ride the horse. On the way back Huw visits Marged-who is unhappy.

Sian Phillips, Sue Jones-Davies

Victoria Plucknett, Keith Drinkel

Jeremy Clyde on horseback

Nerys Hughes, Rhys Powys

Aubrey Richards, Stanley Baker

Nerys Hughes, Sue Jones-Davies, Keith Drinkel

Victoria Plucknett, Keith Drinkel

Bronwen takes Huw to meet Mr. Motshill, head of a new school. After some preliminary questions about math, history, and literature, Huw is accepted and told to report to the school the following Monday.

On Sunday outside the chapel, Evans is waiting to talk to Angharad. Ianto comes along and takes exception to this, knocking Evans flat. Angharad responds by biting her brother on the hand.

When he arrives at school, Huw is set upon by some of the other students, who rough him up and break his pencil box. Mr. Jonas, the teacher, is no help; he berates Huw for being late and in a disheveled condition.

At the conclusion of the day, Huw is once more attacked and beaten. When he returns home, his mother is aghast, but his father is proud of the boy for fighting. Mr. Morgan sends for Dai Bando-a professional fighter-to train Huw in the manly art of boxing.

Victoria Plucknett, Sian Phillips, Rhys Powys

EPISODE 3: HUW'S TRAINING

DIRECTED BY Ronald Wilson   ORIGINAL AIR DATE: January 12, 1976

CAST

Stanley Baker...........Gwilym Morgan
Sian Phillips....................Beth Morgan
Nerys Hughes.........Bronwen Morgan
Norman Comer................Ifor Morgan
Keith Drinkel.................Ianto Morgan
Mike Gwilym...............Owen Morgan
Sue Jones-Davies...Angharad Morgan
Rhys Powys...................Huw Morgan
Dominic Guard..............Huw Morgan
Gareth Thomas.....Reverend Gruffydd
Jeremy Clyde...................Iestin Evans
Ray Smith..........................Dai Bando
John Clive..............................Cyfartha
Victoria Plucknett...................Marged
Aubrey Richards..........................Elias
Clifford Rose.......................Mr. Jonas
Ivor Roberts....................Mr. Motshill
Peter Halliday...............Jack Richards
Robert Blythe..............................Glyn
Malcolm Rogers...........................Will
Michael Griffiths.......Mervyn Phillips

Stanley Baker

Nerys Hughes

Norman Comer

Keith Drinkel

Mike Gwilym

Sue Jones-Davies

Rhys Powys

Sian Phillips

Huw Owen..........................Llewellyn
Yvonne Jones........................Monitor

Dominic Guard   Gareth Thomas

Jeremy Clyde   Ray Smith   John Clive   Victoria Plucknett   Aubrey Richards   Clifford Rose

Ivor Roberts   Peter Halliday   Robert Blythe   Malcolm Rogers   Michael Griffiths   Huw Owen

Dai Bando is up on the high ground teaching Huw how to box. Mrs. Morgan is none too happy about her son fighting. Owen has fixed Huw's pencil box-it looks as good as new.

At school, Mr. Jonas continues to humiliate Huw, especially after the boy pronounces misled "mizzled." Jonas grabs Huw by the ear and further punishes him.

Mike Gwilym, Dominic Guard

Sian Phillips, Rhys Powys

Keith Drinkel, Victoria Plucknett

Family looking somber at the funeral

Miners at the union meeting

Stanley Baker, Norman Comer

Stanley Baker as Gwilym Morgan

Outside Huw and Mervyn Phillips fight; Jonas breaks it up and naturally blames Huw. Instead of telling Mr. Motshill, Jonas decides to make an example of Huw.

In front of the class, Jonas mercilessly flogs Huw with a stick, reducing his back to a raw and bloody pulp. When Huw returns home, his family is appalled.

Mr. Morgan gives Huw five shillings. Dai Bando and his friend Cyfartha are horrified to see the boy's condition, and decide to pay Mr. Jonas a visit.

Iestyn Evans pays a call on Mrs. Morgan, informing her of the incident when he was knocked down on a public footpath by Ianto after speaking to Angharad. Mrs. Morgan had not heard about it.

Marged and Ianto seem to be having a happy day-until their discussion turns to colliery and union business-which Ianto says is very important to him and the other miners.

Next day, Dai Bando and Cyfartha arrive at the school, where they confront Jonas. In the classroom, Dia Bando starts slapping Jonas around, then bends him over the desk and whips him with the same stick he used on Huw, to the applause of the students.

Norman Comer, Nerys Hughes

Huw is getting a severe caning

Ray Smith, Rhys Powys

95

Ray Smith, John Clive

Ray Smith, Stanley Baker

Sian Phillips and Stanley Baker

Mothshill comes along, calling Dai Bando a maniac. Back home, Huw reports the incident to his father, and says he is getting a new teacher. Dai Bando is invited to the Morgan home for dinner.

Although it is pouring rain, Ianto feels he must attend a union meeting, where an important election of officers is to take place. He leaves an unhappy Marged alone.

Marged begins drinking, finishing a bottle, passing out and knocking over a lamp in the process. The house catches on fire, and burns to the ground. Marged is burned to death. Owen takes it particularly hard.

Time passes and Huw grows to near manhood. Iestyn Evans is still interested in Angharad; Mr. Elias is still as cranky as ever. Elias is at odds with Gruffydd, who he thinks should be married.

After reading the minister the riot act, Elias heads out and Angharad comes in. Elias wants to know what she is doing there; she tells the grocer to mind his own business.

Gruffydd tells Anghard she can't go wrong marrying Iestyn Evans, but she says she wants him and not Evans. Gruffydd points out he is twice her age, and only has a salary of £25 a year. He will not subject her to a life of poverty. He thinks too highly of her.

Dai Bando teaches Huw to box

98

Rhys Powys, Sian Phillips, Mike Gwilym

Clifford Rose, Rhys Powys

Stanley Baker, Sian Phillips, Norman Comer, Mike Gwilym,
Rhys Powys

Jeremy Clyde, Sian Phillips

Gareth Thomas, Sue Jones-Davies, Aubrey Richards

John Clive, Ray Smith

The pay of the miners is being cut, and they decide to go on strike. Mr. Morgan is against the strike; he says that everyone should go back to work. He tells his family that the only person making out during the strike is the undertaker.

Huw visits Ivor and Bronwen; he notices the atmosphere in their home is very happy compared to the Morgan house. Meanwhile, old Mr. Evans dies-now Iestyn is the mine owner.

After the miners decide to go back to work, Ianto decides to go to London. Owen goes with him, saying "There's nothing here, boyo." The two brothers have made peace with one another.

Angharad is very upset to see a wedding announcement in The London Times, saying that she and Iestyn have become engaged. This is the first she has heard of it!

Ivor Roberts, Clifford Rose, Ray Smith

Jeremy Clyde, Sue Jones-Davies

EPISODE 4: ANGHARAD ARRIVES

DIRECTED BY Ronald Wilson ORIGINAL AIR DATE: January 19, 1976

CAST

Stanley Baker...........Gwilym Morgan
Sian Phillips...................Beth Morgan
Nerys Hughes.........Bronwen Morgan
Sue Jones-Davies...Angharad Morgan
Jeremy Clyde...................Iestin Evans
Dominic Guard..............Huw Morgan
Norman Comer................Ifor Morgan
Keith Drinkel................Ianto Morgan
Mike Gwilym...............Owen Morgan
Gareth Thomas.....Reverend Gruffydd
Ray Smith..........................Dai Bando
John Clive.............................Cyfartha
Aubrey Richards.........................Elias
Sheila Ruskin.............Blodwen Evans
Rachel Thomas.............Mrs. Nicholas
Zelah Clarke...............Ceinwen Lloyd
Brinley Jenkins...................Mr. Lloyd
John Pierce-Jones..............Mr. Powys

Stanley Baker   Sian Phillips

Nerys Hughes   Sue Jones-Davies

Jeremy Clyde   Dominic Guard

Norman Comer   Keith Drinkel

103

Mike Gwilym	Gareth Thomas	Ray Smith	John Clive	Aubrey Richards	Sheila Ruskin
Rachel Thomas	Zelah Clarke	Brinley Jenkins	John Pierce-Jones	Welsh Singer 1	Welsh Singer 2
Welsh Singer 3	Welsh Singer 4	Welsh Singer 5	Welsh Singer 6	Welsh Singer 7	Welsh Singer 8
Welsh Singer 9	Welsh Singer 10	Welsh Singer 11[	Welsh Singer 12	Welsh Singer 13	Welsh Singer 14
Welsh Singer 15	Welsh Singer 16	Welsh Singer 17	Welsh Singer 18		

Angharad arrives at the Evans estate where she meets Iestyn's sister Blodwen. The angry Angharad demands to know by what right Iestyn put the wedding announcement in the newspaper.

104

Sian Phillips, Norman Comer, Nerys Hughes

Gareth Thomas, Sian Phillips

105

Gareth Thomas & Dominic Guard

Welsh singers practicing

Stanley Baker reads a letter

Evans says that he was confident that she would marry him, even if the announcement was a trifle premature. He then formally proposes, and she accepts.

The Morgans are not quite sure how they feel about the situation. Mr. Gruffydd, who is still moving into his new chapel residence, says that the upcoming marriage is splendid.

However Bronwen notices the pain on Gruffydd's face. Dai Bando, who is helping the minister move in, tells him that between the two of them, they have made Huw Morgan quite a man.

Huw meanwhile is finding himself the centre of attention of a young girl, Cienwen Lloyd. Back at the Evans estate, Iestyn can't wait to sell the house and property, as well as the colliery, and leave the area.

Bronwen visits Mr. Gruffydd and tells him that Angharad is marrying the wrong man, but Gruffydd says he cannot and will not interfere. He says it's God's will.

But Bronwen says he should at least go and talk to Angharad, and get things perfectly clear. But Gruffydd refuses, saying he has no right and it would only lead to misery.

Nerys Hughes as Bronwen Morgan

Stanley Baker as Gwilym Morgan

Sian Phillips & Stanley Baker

Mr. & Mrs. Morgan enjoy a good laugh

109

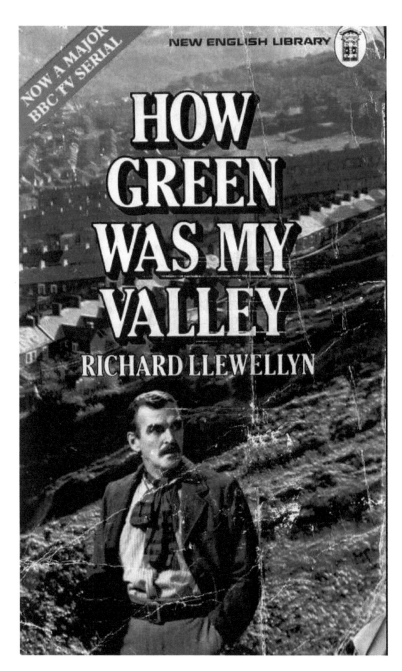

Book Cover

Rachel Thomas, Sue Jones-Davies

Angharad visits Blodwen, and wonders what is going to happen to her after spending her whole life there on the estate. She says she has a small annuity, and may wind up in a little boarding house.

Iestyn still wants to sell and get out of the area, but he makes Angharad a bargain. If she will marry him in London in a private ceremony, he will take the house off the market.

When Angharad tells her parents she will be married in London, they feel they are being snubbed. Mr. Morgan however philosophically states that the change of venue will save a lot of trouble and expense.

Stanley Baker, Sian Phillips

Jeremy Clyde, Sue Jones-Davies

Sue Jones-Davies, Sheila Ruskin

Dominic Guard, Zelah Clarke

Zelah Clarke, Dominic Guard

Mrs. Morgan next invites Mr. Gruffydd home where he can have "a proper tea." She says she is not sure if the upcoming marriage is right. Someone, she says, should have counseled Angharad.

Huw has a heart to heart talk with Gruffydd about Cienwen Lloyd, the girl who is keen on him. In London, Angharad visits her brothers. Ianto is still peeved about the marriage, but Owen agrees to walk her down the aisle.

Norman Comer, Dominic Guard, Sian Phillips

Gareth Thomas, Nerys Hughes

Sheila Ruskin pours some lemonade for Sue Jones-Davies

Aubrey Richards, Sian Phillips

Back in the valley, Ivor is working very hard with his choir of Welsh singers. Everyone bursts with pride when he gets a letter from Buckingham Palace; the choir has been given a Royal Command to sing before Queen Victoria.

Blodwen arrives at the Morgan home inquiring whether anything has been heard from Iestyn and Angharad, who have now married and are on their honeymoon.

After Ivor and the choir get on the train for London, Cienwen arrives and persuades Huw into taking her up a nearby mountain to look for some nightingales.

When it becomes late and Cienwen has not returned home, her father and some others go out looking for her. He's not too happy thinking she may be with a young man.

A foggy day in the valley

Ray Smith, John Clive, Gareth Thomas

EPISODE 5: NIGHT TIME STORY

DIRECTED BY Ronald Wilson   ORIGINAL AIR DATE: January 26, 1976

CAST

Stanley Baker...........Gwilym Morgan
Sian Phillips...................Beth Morgan
Nerys Hughes.........Bronwen Morgan
Norman Comer................Ifor Morgan
Keith Drinkel................Ianto Morgan
Mike Gwilym...............Owen Morgan
Dominic Guard..............Huw Morgan
Gareth Thomas....Reverend Gruffydd
Sue Jones-Davies...Angharad Morgan
Jeremy Clyde...................Iestin Evans
Ray Smith..........................Dai Bando
John Clive.............................Cyfartha
Sheila Ruskin.............Blodwen Evans
Rachel Thomas.............Mrs. Nicholas
Clifford Rose.......................Mr. Jonas
Barbara Bolton..................Ruth Jonas
Zelah Clarke...............Ceinwen Lloyd
Sean Mathias.............................Lloyd
David Lloyd.............................Rhodri
Raymond Bowers...............Cheapjack

Stanley Baker

Sian Phillips

Nerys Hughes   Norman Comer

Keith Drinkel   Mike Gwilym

Dominic Guard   Gareth Thomas

Sue Jones-Davies   Jeremy Clyde   Ray Smith   John Clive   Sheila Ruskin   Rachel Thomas

Clifford Rose   Barbara Bolton   Zelah Clarke   Raymond Bowers   Boy   Vendor

Williams

Huw and Cienwen are out in the woods looking for nightingales. When she goes home, she makes up a story that she went for a walk, got lost, and fell asleep. Mrs. Morgan knows what happened; she tells Huw he is just a kid.

Stanley Baker, Keith Drinkel, Mike Gwilym

Keith Drinkel, Sian Phillips, Mike Gwilym

Mr. Jonas ostracizing a student

Jeremy Clyde, Sue Jones-Davies

Barbara Bolton, Clifford Rose

Norman Comer, Nerys Hughes, Dominic Guard

Ivor and the choir return from a triumphant visit to Windsor Castle. He says Queen Victoria shook his hand, and presented him with a portrait of herself.

Gwilym Morgan is so happy for the success of his son that he goes out to celebrate, returning home quite drunk with Dai Bando and Cyfartha. Mrs. Morgan is very understanding.

On their honeymoon in Europe, Iestyn and Angharad are having a heated discussion; she does not care for his business associates and their behaviour. He tells her to just make the best of it.

Mrs. Morgan is delighted when she receives a letter from Owen and Ianto, informing her they are coming home. Huw, now a senior boy, is still at school. He is now a prefect.

Ray Smith, Stanley Baker, Sian Phillips

John Clive, Ray Smith

Dominic Guard, Nerys Hughes

Keith Drinkel, Mike Gwilym, Dominic Guard

Ray Smith, Dominic Guard

Portrait of Queen Victoria

One of the boys, Williams, has gotten on the bad side of Mr. Jonas-who takes it out on him by his usual stick-beating. Huw remembers his own caning at the hands of Jonas, and punches out the teacher.

Back at the Morgan home, Ianto and Owen return to the delight of Beth and Gwilym. Mr. Morgan says that as long as he lives, they can consider this their home.

Huw goes to Mr. Gruffydd, telling him that he has been expelled from school. His parents don't know yet, and Huw fears the news will break his mother's heart. Gruffydd says he will intervene with headmaster Mr. Motshill and see if anything can be done.

When he does so, Mothshill tells him that it would be a shame for Huw not to be able to take his exams, but he remains expelled from the school. With this compromise, Jonas will not press charges.

Dominic Guard, Stanley Baker

Norman Comer, Nerys Hughes

Sue Jones-Davies, Sheila Ruskin

Mike Gwilym, Sheila Ruskin

Sian Phillips, Stanley Baker

Ray Smith & Sian Phillips

Huw decides to go to see Jonas to apologize, but when he arrives, Jonas is less than cordial. He tells Huw that the two of them were like oil and water right from the first time Huw came to the school.

Jonas' sister Ruth says that her brother is really a good man, but Huw sees him as a troubled sadist. Apparently Jonas came from the same origins as Huw, but bettered himself, wanting Huw to do the same. At least that's how Ruth tells it.

Sian Phillips, Stanley Baker

Nerys Hughes, Norman Comer, Sian Phillips

Sian Phillips looking happy

Angharad is getting tired of living in hotels; she wants to return to Wales and live in a proper house. When Iestyn tells her he has sold the colliery-which is to be closed down-Angharad becomes angry, as this will put 400 men out of work.

Gwilym worries that he will be unemployed, but Beth tells him that they are strong people and will be able to survive. They will just have to tighten their belts and make some adjustments.

Gareth Thomas, Dominic Guard

Blodwen Evans pays a visit-she is ashamed that her brother has sold the colliery and caused a sticky situation, but Mrs. Morgan says it is not her fault.

They harbour no ill will against her, but Ianto, who is there, has a different view. He storms out of the house after telling Blodwen off. Owen, who comes in later, wonders what just happened.

Huw passes his exams with flying colours. Everyone is proud of him, including Gruffydd. But Huw, knowing the situation, decides to forgo further studies, and go down the mines to help the family financial position.

EPISODE 6: BRONWEN GRIEVES

DIRECTED BY Ronald Wilson ORIGINAL AIR DATE: February 2, 1976

CAST

Stanley Baker...........Gwilym Morgan
Sian Phillips...................Beth Morgan
Nerys Hughes.........Bronwen Morgan
Sue Jones-Davies...Angharad Morgan
Dominic Guard..............Huw Morgan
Gareth Thomas.....Reverend Gruffydd
Keith Drinkel.................Ianto Morgan
Mike Gwilym...............Owen Morgan
Sheila Ruskin.............Blodwen Evans
Ray Smith.........................Dai Bando
John Clive.............................Cyfartha
Aubrey Richards.........................Elias
Rachel Thomas.............Mrs. Nicholas
Peter Halliday...............Jack Richards
Zelah Clarke...............Ceinwen Lloyd
Jack Walters...................Will Hopkins
Philip Joseph.....................Evan Johns
Sion Probert...............................Gwyn
Matthew Comer.........................Gareth
Benjamin Turley.....................Taliesin
Clive Roberts............................Miner

Stanley Baker   Sian Phillips

Nerys Hughes   Sue Jones-Davies

Dominic Guard   Gareth Thomas

Keith Drinkel   Mike Gwilym

133

Sheila Ruskin   Ray Smith   John Clive   Aubrey Richards   Rachel Thomas   Peter Halliday

Zelah Clarke   Jack Walters   Philip Joseph   Sion Probert   Matthew Comer   Little Boy

Miner   Woman 1   Woman 2

When Ivor is killed in a mine accident, Mrs. Morgan goes to Bronwen and invites her to live in the Morgan house. Bronwen, who is expecting another child, politely refuses.

Sheila Ruskin & Keith Drinkel

Television Poster

Stanley Baker, Mike Gwilym, Keith Drinkel

Sian Phillips, Sheila Ruskin, Sue Jones-Davies

Gwilym looks at Huw for the last time

Ianto is working at an ironworks, and Owen has a job with a blacksmith. Anghard is back in Wales, and Owen volunteers to go and see her. He really wants to see Blodwen.

When he arrives, he apologizes to Blodwen for any untoward remarks made to her by his brother Ianto. He and the rest of the Morgans do not blame Blodwen for her brother's actions.

Huw sees off Cienwen at the train station; she is heading to London to seek her fortune as a stage actress. When Huw returns home, he shares a meal with Owen and Ianto.

Mrs. Morgan is worried about Bronwen; her depression after Ivor's death may lead to her own, Beth feels. She suggests to Huw that he go and live with her.

Sian Phillips & Stanley Baker

Peter Halliday, Dominic Guard, Nerys Hughes

Stanley Baker and Sian Phillips

Nerys Hughes, Sian Phillips

Dominic Guard, Gareth Thomas

Mike Gwilym, Keith Drinkel

Stanley Baker, Philip Joseph, Sion Probert

John Clive, Ray Smith, Keith Drinkel

Huw first goes to visit Angharad, who is as usual home alone; her husband spends little time with her. She does not wish to come home-even for a visit.

Huw tells her that Mr. Gruffydd is still in the village, but he has a heavy heart. When Huw later visits him, he tells Gruffydd that Angharad is also miserable.

Dai Bando, now out of work in the mines, has returned to boxing. Unfortunately during a recent match (which he won), he suffered a blow on the side of the head, which has left him blind.

After Ianto discovers this, he heads home to tell his parents. Unfortunately Blodwen is there, and Ianto tears into her after she says she is sorry.

Stanley Baker reading the paper

Mike Gwilym, Rachel Thomas, Sheila Ruskin

Mike Gwilym, Sheila Ruskin

Stanley Baker, Sian Phillips

Dominic Guard, Sian Phillips

Sian Phillips, Stanley Baker

He says that if Iestyn had not closed most of the mining operations, Dai Bando would not have had to resume his boxing career, and would not have been blinded. As usual, he storms off after the diatribe.

On Owen's next visit to his sister, he takes Mr. Gruffydd along with him. His presence seems to do a world of good both to Angharad as well as Gruffydd.

Dominic Guard, Sue Jones-Davies

Sian Phillips as Beth Morgan

Angharad then gets a surprise visit from her mother. Beth tells her daughter that Owen and Ianto are going to America. Blodwen is going too-she and Owen are to marry next week. Mrs. Morgan sees that Angharad is very unhappy.

Austere housekeeper Mrs. Nicholas seems unmoved and nonplussed about everything-although she is quite a gossip-telling curmudgeonly grocer Mr. Elias all the goings on.

When one of the miners begins courting Bronwen, Huw doesn't like it. He has always had feelings for Bronwen, even though she was the wife of his brother.

Dia Bando has meanwhile found employment in a pub; he seems to be getting on quite well. Gruffydd is now making regular visits to Angharad. Gossipy people begin spreading vitriol.

Keith Drinkel as Ianto Morgan

Mr. Elias, never one to be shy, spreads the manure around. When Gruffydd hears the gossip, he makes a point of giving a sermon on the evils of small-minded people. He then decides to leave the valley.

Conditions in the mine are worsening-a non-operative pump is making things unsafe, and the mine is flooding. At the pub, the men discuss the situation.

Gwilym Morgan decides to take things into his own hands, and fix the pump. When he is in there, the mine caves in, trapping him under a huge slide.

When Gwilym is late, Dai Bando and Huw decide to go into the mine, where they are able to rescue one man, but unfortunately Gwilym has been crushed, and dies just as Huw gets to him.

Gareth Thomas, Sue Jones-Davies

CPSIA information can be obtained
at www.ICGtesting.com
Printed in the USA
BVHW021435160922
647216BV00005B/409